Misbuilding

FUNCTION AND DESIGN

DAVID DREW

Illustrated by Robert Roennfeldt

RIGBY

Find and fix the mistakes.

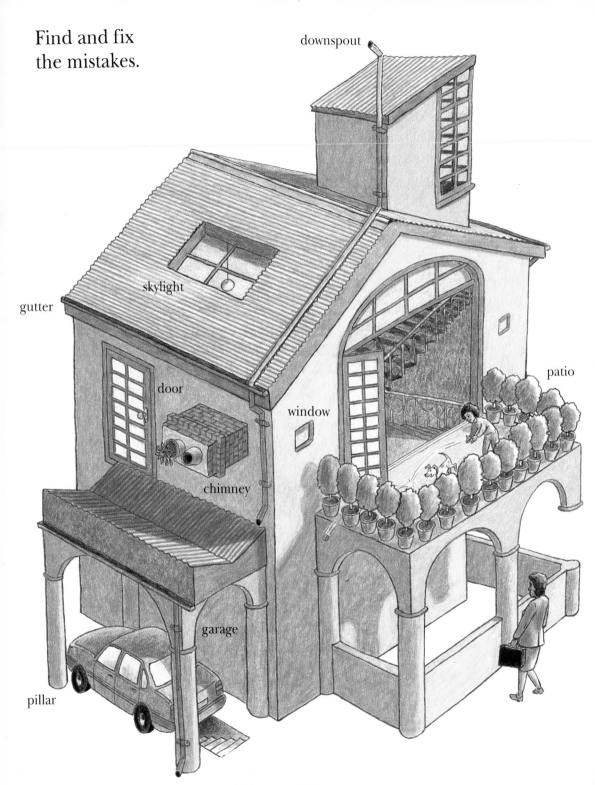

downspout

skylight

gutter

door

window

patio

chimney

garage

pillar

THE HOUSE

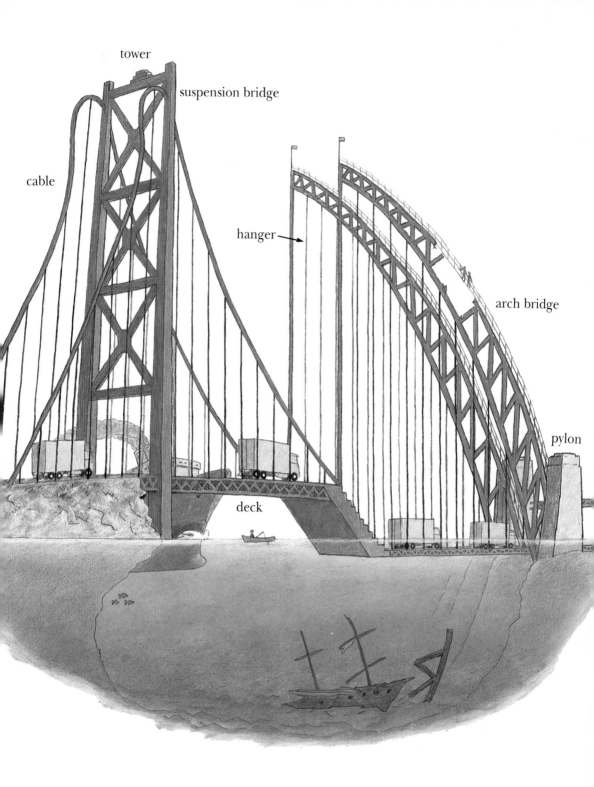

tower

suspension bridge

cable

hanger →

arch bridge

pylon

deck

THE BRIDGE

Find and fix
the mistakes.

armchair

platform

trapdoor

birdhouse

ladder

THE TREEHOUSE

trash can

rope

chain

platform

slide

rings

seat

swing

THE PLAYGROUND

Find and fix the mistakes.

fire escape

trash can

laundry room

bathroom

living room

bedroom

stairs

mail boxes

pillar

front door

THE APARTMENT BLOCK

toll booth

TOLL $1

TOLL BOOTH AHEAD
MERGE RIGHT

EXIT

crosswalk

overpass

sign

THE FREEWAY

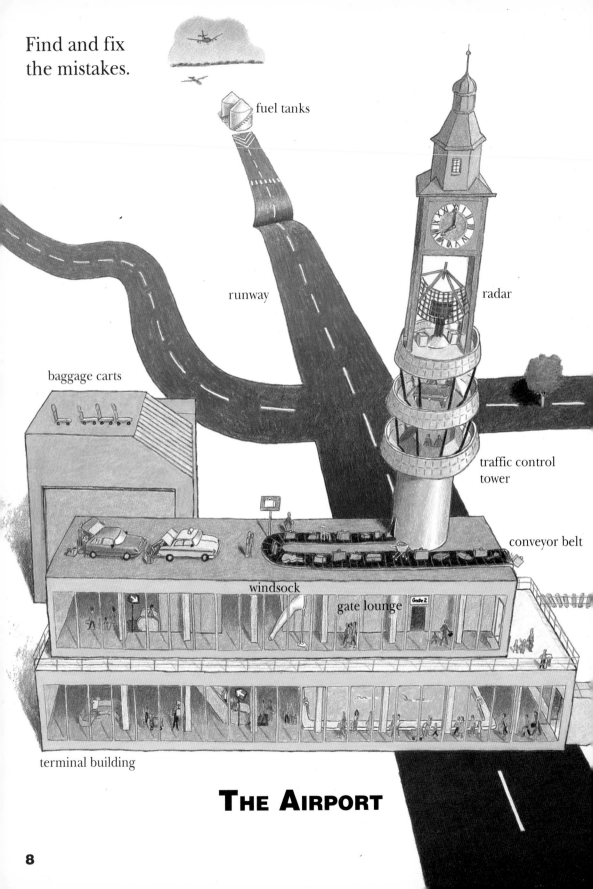

Find and fix
the mistakes.

fuel tanks

runway

radar

baggage carts

traffic control
tower

conveyor belt

windsock

gate lounge

Gate 2

terminal building

THE AIRPORT

THE AIRPLANE

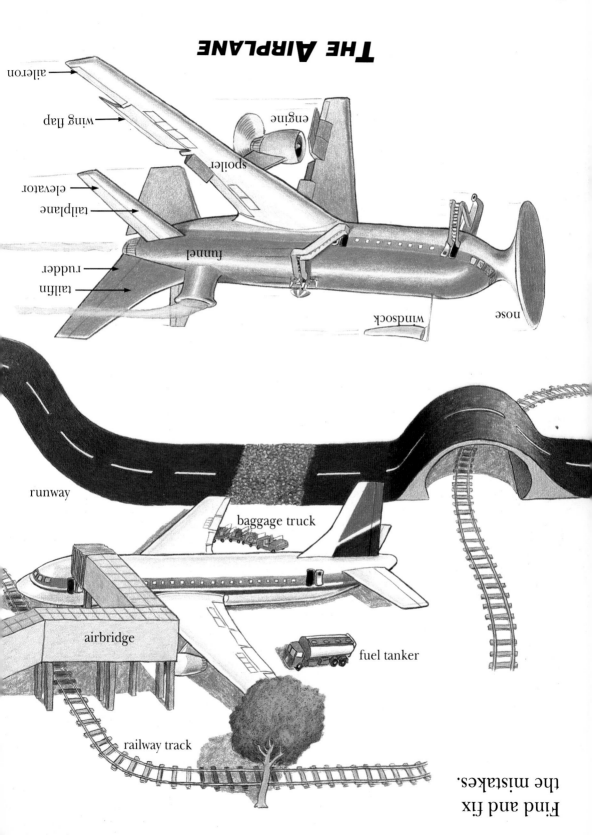

aileron

wing flap

engine

spoiler

elevator

tailplane

funnel

rudder

tailfin

windsock

nose

runway

baggage truck

airbridge

fuel tanker

railway track

Find and fix
the mistakes.

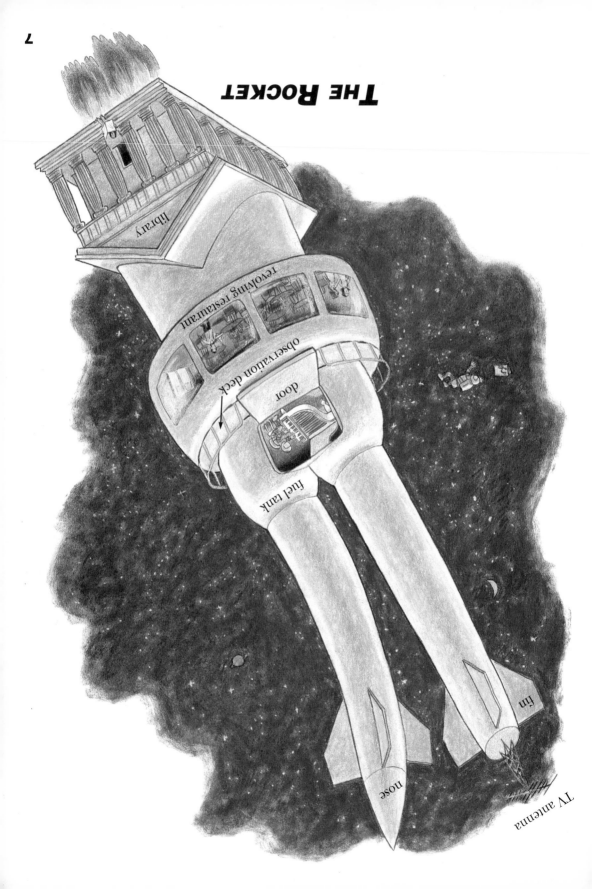

The Helicopter

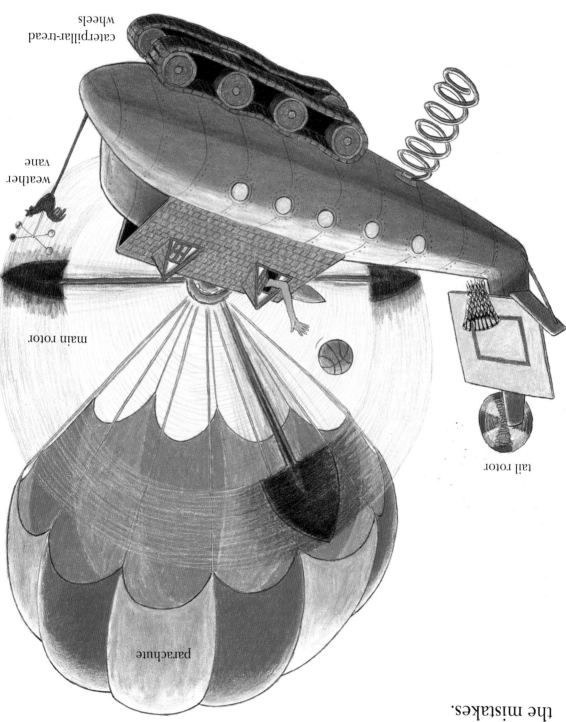

caterpillar-tread wheels

weather vane

main rotor

tail rotor

parachute

Find and fix the mistakes.

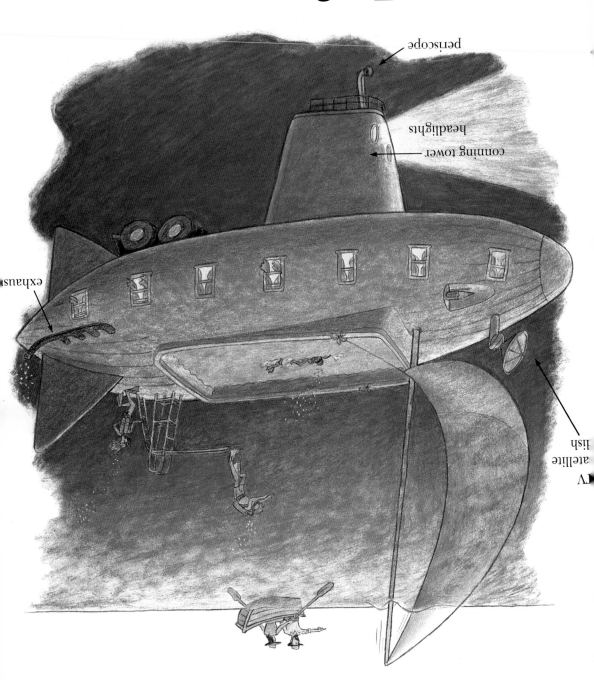

THE SUBMARINE

periscope

headlights

conning tower

exhaust

TV
satellite
dish

THE SAILBOAT

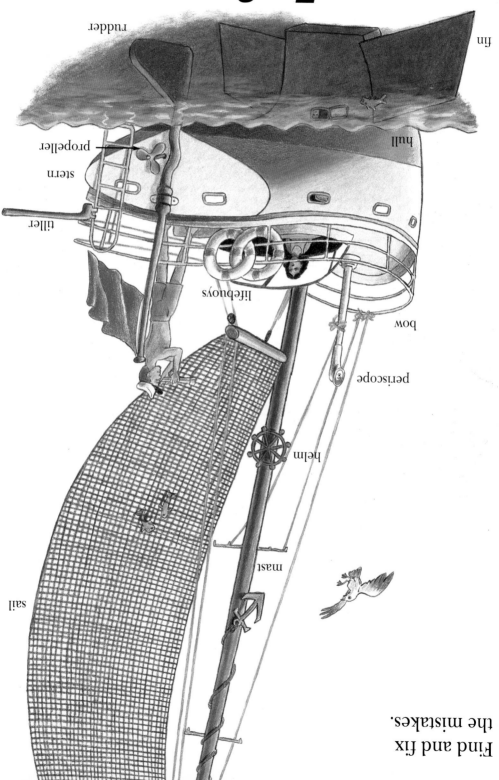

rudder

fin

propeller

hull

stern

tiller

lifebuoys

bow

periscope

helm

mast

sail

Find and fix
the mistakes.

3

The Train

caboose

locomotive

boiler

tunnel

ICE CREAM

GASOLINE

The Bus

bumper

windshield
wiper

fuel tank

DIESEL ONLY

doors

JUPITER
VIA MARS

rotor

passenger car

BAKING
FLOUR

Find and fix
the mistakes.

RIGBY

Illustrated by Robert Roennfeldt

DAVID DREW

FUNCTION AND DESIGN

Untransport